Common House Creatures, Pests, and Irritants

Written by Cathleen Trotter
Illustrated by Sherise McKinney

www.mascotbooks.com

Common House Creatures, Pests, and Irritants

Cover Illustration Copyright © Sherise Mckinney
Book design and production by Greg Martin
Digital/Scanning Services by Randy Fountain
Editing by Andi Kirkman

For more information, please contact:
Mascot Books
560 Herndon Parkway #120
Herndon, VA 20170
info@mascotbooks.com

Library of Congress Control Number: 2016906220
CPSIA Code: PBANG0516A
ISBN: 978-1-63177-585-7

For Brad, Riley, and Talon — thank you for your support and
encouragement. I love you. This book is dedicated to our librarians,
teachers, and lunch ladies and gentlemen; thank you for providing
comfort, stability, and a quiet place to dream.

- **Cathleen**

Thank you to my husband Bryan, who always has my back when I say,
"I have an idea." Thank you to my kids, Brady, Will, and Lorelei for
helping me to capture and care for many of these creatures. This
book is dedicated to the underdogs, the misfits, and the square
pegs everywhere.

- **Sherise**

INTRODUCTION

How to introduce our creatures?
They are who they are —
their intentions vary
in the shaded
grey spectrum
of unbalanced betweens.
These creatures need you
to wonder and dream -
Remember:
look with open eyes
but
see with your smarts
all that is there
and
all that is not.

POP
A MOSTLY HARMLESS GRUMP
& RECLUSIVE COUCH CREATURE

Wedged tight and angry
in the spaces
between places
of
forgotten things…

Lonely.
Mean.
Testy and Pokey.
He surfaces nightly
to snatch crumbs
from
cushy, cushion tops.

**HUMAN, BEWARE -
HANDS, TAKE CARE.**

Invade his space?
Just. Do. Not.

THE WHISPERWORRY
CHRONIC CLOCK WATCHER
& BELEAGUERED BEDTIME CREATURE

Oh, the **BILLS!!!**
The bills are not yet paid!
And tomorrow?
Tomorrow will be insane!
Chores left undone,
things left unsaid —
Inexhaustible aches
of heart, belly, and head.

Really, silly?
You think you should be in bed?
Why even bother? It's already 2 am!
We have moments to ponder
and things to replay;
How long this will take,
I cannot rightly say.

But just maybe,
my fidgety jumpeties could be appeased
were you to hold me and give such a squeeze...

...yawn...

that sleep would come gently
for you and for me,
swaddling us close and surrounding with ease.

SCAPH

BEGRIMED BATHROOM PEST

Scaph, in a sinuous glide,
rounds the still damp tub
scratching her grimy fins
with a swirling whirlpool scrub.
She decides to try her tail
at a little toothpaste art.
She smears the pale, textured paste
in sweeping, minty arcs,
adding depth with goopy globs
in the style of Plop Creature Art.
The toilet paper roll
rocks empty in its cradle.
Scaph crams and stuffs
the two-ply sheets
into the commode
to watch tissue twisters
dance inside the bowl.

A spinning dive as Scaph departs
into the drain's slurp-y bergle.

Dream Snackers
MIDNIGHT NOSHERS & VEXING VAPORS

Dream Snackers congregate, hungrily
hovering above your head,
watching and waiting, longingly
for your dreams to coalesce, deliciously
into streams of **REM**.

With a smack of their wisps
the snackers dig in,
slurping your noodly scenes–
tomorrow you'll wake groggily
to dreams with missing seams.

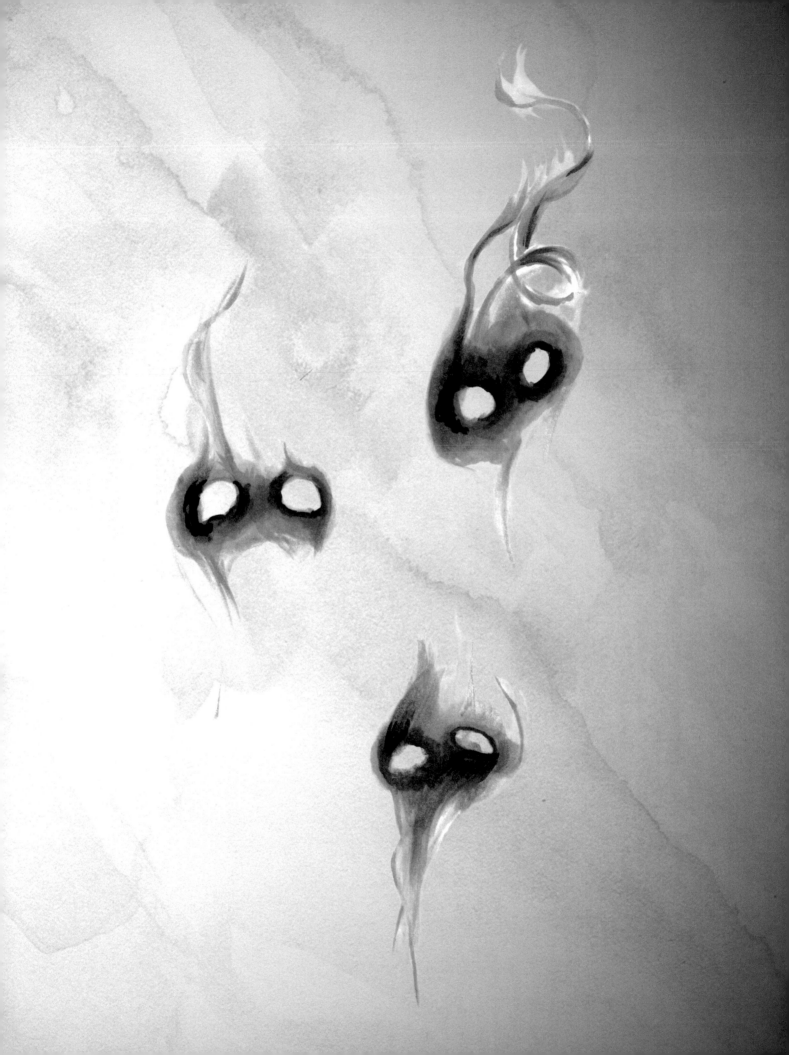

Plin

DOMICILE DECONSTRUCTOR
& CYCLONIC CHAOS CREATURE

The laundry baskets explode
in a burst from within,
and the contents coat the floor like lava.

Dad's resounding screams
shower furiously in between
the swirls of an instigative FLUSH!

The house berserker, Plin,
swipes and then swaps
toys from their spots
to watch the accusations fly.

Plin understands
the domestic demands
that plague family life daily.
He prefers to reject
the banal concept
that is your well-kept dwelling.

OPAL
CHEERY CONSTANT & HEARTENED HELPER

Bright-eyed morning creature,
Collector of the sun,
Opal provides threads of hope
when you're ragged, seeping,
and worn.

A litany of positivity
in times of ceaseless weeping.
She delivers, in smatters,
these daily rays of truth:
You, sweet one, do matter
and **YES**, you are enough.

Remember to keep ever forward
and watch out for the ruts.

Strüdel

Famished Finisher & Secret Snacker

Wait!!! Where…
the last slice of cake
sat all scrumptious and yummy
and wickedly beckoned
with delicate frosting
AND that glory-filled donut
with the delectable, sticky glaze
waited temptingly for ME–
but sadly…**I'm TOO LATE!!!**

From the last of the granola
and candy type bars
to that one feisty pickle
swimming solo in the jar,
all of the just ones
have inexplicably disappeared!
But the echo of wrappers,
discarded and crammed,
crinkle rather loudly
from wherever they're jammed.

The culprit is Strüdel:
Eater of the Only,
the Last,
and Just Ones.

POCKET

**ABSCONDER OF TOOLS
& MASTER OF MECHANICAL MISCHIEF**

Greasy garage pest
that stealthily slinks
while the mechanic performs
all types of maintenance.

Pocket swipes tools
that were carefully just placed
by callused and bleeding hands.

He bumps the light stands,
unplugs the air compressor,
and distributes motor oil liberally.
With grabby little paws,
Pocket appropriates
wrenches and tape measures,
hiding them in random places.

Pocket stops and stares -
the mechanic's in the middle
of a glorious meltdown -
all rant-y and rave-y,
face flushed
a pulsing, angry red.
Behold the eyes
boiling with rage.
Pocket takes the hint
and scampers away.

SPANNER

HOARD OF THE LAUNDRY

He hides somewhere
behind the dryer
just past the bluish green lint.
Midnight excursions
of mayhem commence
when this solitary irritant
roams from his nest,
a hidden lost and found of sorts.
Spanner dives into the piles
of neatly folded clothes,
stacked, waiting for departure.
He also rearranges
the presorted rainbow
of laundry waiting its turn.
Spanner throws detergent
here and also there
burying the scoop like treasure.
He eats one half
of the smelly sock pair,
stuffing the other in a corner.
Spanner stops the dryer
and silences the washer,
muttering about beeps and clinking metal.
Your towels, unfinished,
begin to sour
and your shirts will be horribly wrinkled.
Spanner bids the quiet
laundry room goodnight
and retires to a peaceful slumber.

THE THING ON THE STAIRS
SURREPTITIOUS STALKER & PREMEDITATING PEST

Silently it stalks,
The Thing on the Stairs
merely a step or two behind
like your shadow, It follows you.
Murmurs of hot breath
tremble down your spine.
Deliberately, It inches closer
and closer still
to an unaware you
Until
a moan sounds
from not so far below-
instantly you know…
suddenly you hear
alarming noises drawing,
drawing **VERY** near!
It chases you higher,
as faster you flee
a quick backward glance
not quite sure
what you may see,
yet unease persists
as limbs of snatchery
make a grab for your feet-
AAaaaHhh…lucky for you,
you've reached the top and
The Thing on the Stairs
can do nothing
but **STOMP**
and **STOMP**
and **STOMP** some more,
as It descends,
dejectedly, down
into
the basement
below.

Yawp

POUTY PEST & CLEVER HOUSE CREATURE

Here's a little pest
who appears quite helpless
and rather lost.
Annoyingly whiny,
is this one named Yawp.
You see,
he hasn't any hands
and he isn't very tall,
BUT
he's smart enough to know
the most magical word of all:

Mom!
M-o-o-o-o-m!!
M-o-o-o-o-o-o-o-o-m!!!
Will you come?
Come, please and HELP!

Then, as patiently (or pestily) as possible
wait…wait…
aaannd **POOF!**
The one they call **MOM**
arrives in a **SWOOSH!**
She straightens, fixes, calms, and such
always responding
whatever the fuss (however much muck!)
That's how little ones
no matter the kind
get food in their bellies
and socks on their feet
and really, most anything that falls in between.

The Harrower

LACHRYMOSE LANGUISHER

The Harrower abruptly appears
in the midst of your emotional
quicksand,
Where, during **THOSE** days,
you're forced to remain
stagnantly in the past
drowning heavily in the refrain…

and
Where melancholic puffs
accompany long-dismissed 'was'
in the trenches
of 'Oh, what-have-I-dones'.

Directly, the Harrower
encircles,
narrows,
expelling ages of pain.

THE HUTCHBRUME
INQUISITIVE OBSCURITY

A staticky haze
formlessly roams
misting through the realms
of shadow-filled rooms.
Curious, peering,
The Hutchbrume
flickers,
sifts,
settles in the corner.

BILLOW
HARMLESS BLANKET HOG
& NOCTURNAL BED CREATURE

A
sweetie of a beastie
nestled within a rolling,
wrestling ocean of blankets.
Softly.
Calmly.
Snuggly.
Ever tug,
tug,
tugging
the blankets
from your side
so that she may rest within
the stolen comforter,
warmly doing its job.

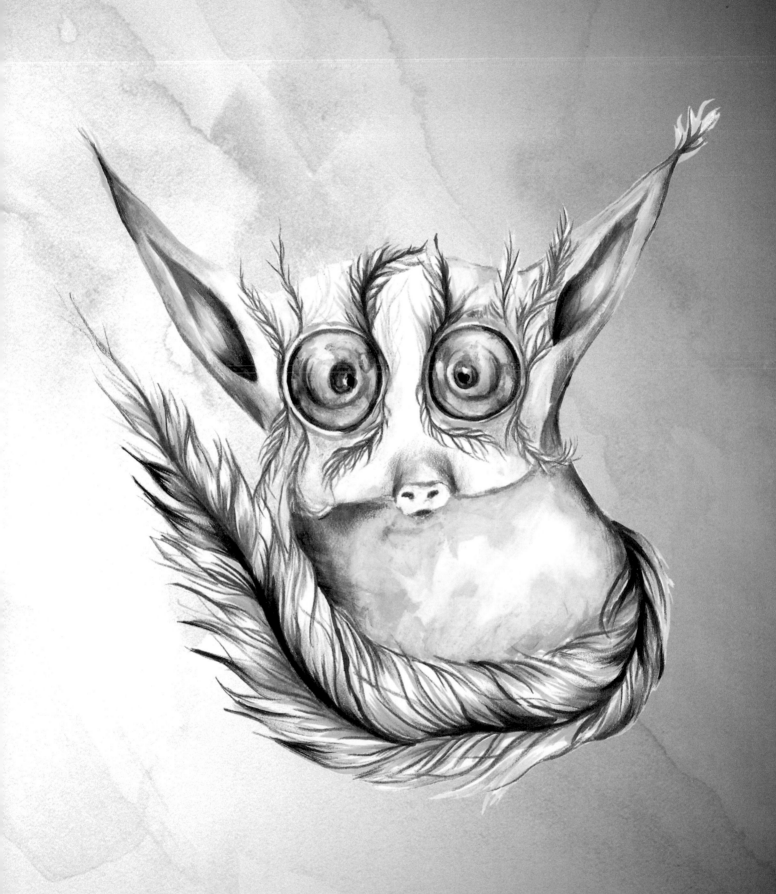

THE DELATORIO
DEVILISH DUO & INIQUITOUS IRRITANTS

The Deletorio Twins are notorious schemers
and masters of orchestrated pain.
They reposition the furniture
and realign sharp edges,
assuring maximum damages be applied
to the knees, toes, bony elbows,
and that sensitive spot on your side.

The Deletorio scatter blocks
and tiny, sharp toys
strategically on the floor.
Nefariously they watch
you plod unaware
directly onto their trap.
Furiously you roar,
one-foot-hopping
in retreat
to the door.

Your pain and suffering viciously delight
this notorious, devilish duo.
Caution is imperative
when creeping at night;
Heed the Deletorio's gauntlet.

THE SLACKEN
PROFESSIONAL PROCRASTINATOR
& INDIFFERENT IRRITANT

Psstt…
Um, your favorite shows (**OF ALL TIME!**)
are playing on the tube,
marathon style, a bingeworthy view.
Sooo you needn't bother
with chores or must-do's,
because those tedious items
await, indelibly unchecked
on a list, specifically for you.

Why start now, why finish early
when more to-do's linger
eagerly, vying for a spot.
Speaking of which, the Slacken sits
comfy and cozy, ensconced
in the couch, warming a place
for you to recline with snacks and treats,
saving the drudgery for later.

The Slacken quietly wraps
around your ability to verb
and gently props your feet.
It's time to burrow
for hours and hours
and leave those pesky, hurried things
waiting,
for tomorrow's tomorrow.

NIMIUS
PANIC PROMPTER & ANXIETY BOOSTER

A knot materializes,
taut and angry,
causing your neck to scream.

Panic-swollen, it ruptures –
Nimius emerges
in ooze-coated anxiety.
Terror infects everyday thoughts.
Corrupted, they pinball wildly,
arcing inside your brain.
Thoughts cleave incoherently
and form a maddening loop.

A universe of obligations,
worry and sorrow rain down,
disappointments are endless,
reactive I can'ts bound,
to infinite what ifs–
and dreadful why, why-now's.

These weighted misconceptions
incessantly repeat,
rendering you unsteady.
Tightly constricted and tethered in place,
you struggle to break free and flee.

AGGER
HYPOCHONDRIAC ENABLER

Are you pale?
A tad bit feverish?
Your eyes are glassy
and you look sort of peaked.
Perhaps it's a cold?
It may be the FLU
or that rather thorough virus
circulating about school.
Ugh!
Do you recall, recently
pushing the grocery cart
so carefree
without any thought
to germs and communicability?
Infectious disease for everyone!
(Perhaps bacterial in nature)
Hurry! To the WEB.
Self-diagnosis looms within
tiny, clickable boxes.
Oh! This sudden,
blinding migraine
pulsing inside your brain
is most likely a tumor
or
Mmmhmm -
Eyestrain.
That pressure in your chest
could be a heart attack,
or better yet
a case of severe indigestion.
Oops.
Nope.
Clearly, you suffer
the Gas.

CEDE

INHIBITOR OF CREATIVE ARTISTRY

A jab -
Sting!
Hesitation unfurls.
Its tendrils, seek.
Your creativity
once caught
suffocates
in the sump
of sticky, self-doubt
The true poison seeps -
Self-Defeating Stasis.

MURREN
FIENDISH FOOT GRABBER

A running start
heart-thumping leap
thunderous WHUMP
bedframe creaks.

Careful now, tuck with haste
all your limbs
and hide your face!

Tuck the edges nice and tight
keep yourself
from Murren's sight.

Safe inside an exhaled cocoon
blanketed magic
hot CO_2.

TWITCH
NEEDY NUISANCE
& PATHOLOGICAL TICKLER

Barely-there strands of hair
lingering lightly, whispers on skin.

You know it's there
somewhere, but WHERE?
Perhaps on your arm? No, wait! Your leg?
Invisible strings forever dangling.

Search and search
and search you will
for phantom tingles
that will not still
or ever cease!

Unless,
of course,
you hug this beast..